IS MOTHER
NATURE
MAD?

IS MOTHER NATURE MAD?

*How to Work with
Nature Spirits to Mitigate
Natural Disasters*

Elizabeth Clare Prophet

Summit University ♨ Press®

IS MOTHER NATURE MAD?
*How to Work with Nature Spirits to Mitigate
Natural Disasters*
by Elizabeth Clare Prophet
Copyright © 2008 Summit Publications, Inc.
All rights reserved

For information, contact Summit University Press,
63 Summit Way, Gardiner, MT 59030.
Tel: 1-800-245-5445 or 406-848-9500
www.SummitUniversityPress.com

Library of Congress Control Number: 2008923281
ISBN: 978-1-932890-13-6

SUMMIT UNIVERSITY 🦢 PRESS

Cover design by George Foster www.fostercovers.com
Some images © 2008 Jupiterimages Corporation

DISCLAIMER: No guarantee is made by Summit University Press that
the practice of the Science of the Spoken Word®, meditation, visualization,
prayers, mantras or fiats will yield any person's desired results. The func-
tioning of cosmic law is a direct experience between the individual and his
own higher consciousness. We can only witness to our personal experiences
through the use of any suggested mantras or spiritual disciplines. The spiritual practices set forth herein are not intended to—and must not—replace
appropriate medical treatment or commonsense methods of self-protection,
including avoidance of potentially dangerous situations.

Printed in the United States of America.
13   12   11   10   09   08   6   5   4   3   2   1

Contents

PART 1

The Link between Mankind and Nature

Robert's Story

In January 2007, Australia was in the midst of its worst drought in history. Farmers were suffering tremendous hardships. Suicide rates were up in country towns. Reservoirs and rivers were running dry. Newspapers were writing about global warming and doomsday scenarios.

In the midst of this, a group of fifty or so people from all over the continent assembled for a five-day seminar. One of the topics was how to work with nature spirits to break the drought.

In a two-hour workshop, we learned how the forces of nature mirror man's thoughts and feelings and that physical drought may be the result of a drought, a dearth, in people's consciousness. We also learned spiritual techniques to work with nature spirits: to send them love, to send them a clear mental image *of what we would like them to manifest, and to pray for them scientifically.*

For five days we practiced these techniques midst the glorious, sunny weather of an Australian East Coast summer. And then it rained. In some places it poured. The weather map showed rain across the continent from coast to coast—particularly in some areas hardest hit by the drought. Some outback areas even had floods. But residents were happy to think of the new life that the rain would bring.

Experts analyzed what had happened. They talked about this rain possibly marking the end of the El Niño weather pattern that had caused the drought. Much more rain would be needed in most areas, but there seemed to be hope.

Was this all a coincidence? Was the rain just the result of impersonal natural forces, which, if we only knew enough about them, could be predicted? Or was it an example of what a few people could do if they learned to work consciously with nature spirits?

 Is Mother Nature Mad?

This was the headline from a local newspaper one snowy day in December 1996 as 90 mph winds and heavy rain and snow pummeled the northwest United States, causing roofs to buckle, power lines to go down and avalanches to block major highways. The headline—and the question—was more perceptive than many of us realize.

Since then, the elements have only become more capricious and unpredictable. In recent years, we've seen a staggering number of severe storms and floods. Hurricanes and tornadoes. Earthquakes and tsunamis. Heat waves, droughts, fires and volcanic eruptions. Natural disasters have resulted in a tremendous loss of life and resources.

A Wake-Up Call

*W*hy all the eccentric behavior? I believe it's related to the law of cause and effect, which operates throughout our lives. This law decrees that our thoughts, words and deeds—positive and negative—create a chain reaction and that we will personally experience the effect of every cause we have set in motion. We are responsible for our actions as well as the effect they have on ourselves and all other parts of life, including the nature kingdom.

So the law of cause and effect, also known as karma, is what we're seeing outpictured in the unusual and calamitous manifestations of nature. We are largely responsible for what is happening to our earth and the ecosystem. Therefore we are reaping our karma of the past.

There are so many problems in the world—starvation on the planet,

> *In nature there are neither rewards nor punishments—there are consequences.*
>
> — ROBERT GREEN INGERSOLL

drugs in the streets, all kinds of violence. And then we have erratic weather patterns and natural disasters. I do not see these events as unrelated. They are related. They are related, and we are, in part, responsible.

This is a message deep within the soul; we know it internally. But when we don't respond to our inner awareness and to the inner direction we may receive, then sooner or later, one way or another, the karma descends. It descends so that we will pause, come together to deal with the situation, and reflect on what life is truly all about.

So these disasters are waking people up— they're awakening to the flame of the heart, to love and compassion, and they're pulling together. But we are still facing significant problems, and many of them are interrelated.

 A Chain Reaction

Looking at the roots of Mother Nature's frenzy, we find that on the physical level the abuse of the environment through deforestation, the widespread burning of fossil fuels, acid rain and all kinds of pollution has created a chain reaction we never anticipated. The risks we have taken with our environment are big ones, and we have no idea where the chain reaction will end.

But the physical abuse of the environment is only one side of the story—the visible side. If we want to understand the traumas playing out before us, we need to look beyond the veil to the nature kingdom and the largely invisible burdens we have placed upon it. We need to see beyond the outer symptoms to the inner cause.

 # Levels of Consciousness in Nature

When we look at the visible world through the filter of scientific knowledge, we may think that things happen without an intelligence directing them. And yet, when a natural disaster wreaks havoc in our lives, we call it an act of God or, simply, nature. What is nature? And does nature have an intelligence, a consciousness?

From the most distant stars to the smallest dewdrop, the universe is tended by innumerable invisible hands. Angels guide and guard us and minister to our needs. Enlightened spiritual beings, in the planes of Spirit, teach our souls and illumine the way back to our Source. And nature spirits, also known as "elementals," tend the forces of nature in the elements of fire, air, water and earth.

To the illumined mind the whole world burns and sparkles with light.

— RALPH WALDO EMERSON

The elementals work with the mineral, vegetable and animal kingdoms, and all these have some form of consciousness. There is, however, a great difference in the level of consciousness of each group.

The mineral kingdom doesn't possess self-awareness but rather a quality of mineral density and spiritual radiance that is imparted to each element and particle through the consciousness of the nature spirits. The elementals also administer the divine pattern for each rock, precious stone and component of mineral life.

Trees and plants have imparted to them a

greater degree of life awareness than that of the mineral kingdom. Studies show that plants experience sensations, emit sound, and react to their surroundings and to factors such as people, music and emotions. All plant life is tended by nature spirits, which impart to everything that grows the sensitivity that scientists record. Kirlian photography, for instance, has documented the life force in plants, revealing an aura of universal energy, an electromagnetic field, which is also common to man and animals.

Animals and sea creatures possess still higher levels of consciousness and intelligence. They may display characteristics that seem almost human as well as an uncanny intuitive sense and attunement. Indeed, a marvelous attunement and interrelatedness exists everywhere in nature.

> *In some mysterious way woods have never seemed to me to be static things. In physical terms, I move through them; yet in metaphysical ones, they seemed to move through me.*
>
> – JOHN FOWLES

A Monarch Butterfly

It was time to do some weeding in my garden and I did it by putting both my hands in the soil. The sun came shining through the clouds. The bees and bumblebees buzzed around my head. I forgot about time, and I felt one with nature all around me.

When I was finished, I raked everything together that had been weeded out. Having done this, I saw out of the corner of my eye a beautiful monarch butterfly sitting on the edge of my wooden barn. I felt childlike excitement and a great sense of peace and love.

I moved my right hand slowly towards the butterfly until I was very close to its little front legs. I waited patiently. Then it stepped with one leg on my finger, then the second leg, the third, fourth, fifth and sixth.

I admired it from all sides and told it, silently, how beautiful it was. As if the butterfly felt my admiration, it suddenly raised its wings and I could see its left eye and its fluffy little body. Then it lowered its wings and

*I could see the stunning colors on top of them.
After a while, I walked over to a large bush
with violet flowers and it stepped lightly onto
one of them.*

Unseen Friends and Helpers

Tending all these levels of life, the elementals have left their footprints in the lore and legend of many cultures, where they are described as everything from playful fairies and sprites to mischievous elves and leprechauns to grumpy gnomes. Many young children, because they have so recently come from the heaven-world and therefore can see invisible realms with their inner sight, have adopted these little folk as their "imaginary" playmates. Most grownups, however, don't see nature spirits or recall having interacted with them as children.

A Little Friend Comes in the Door

This little girl was watching out to make sure that her "imaginary" friend didn't get left behind.

One day my four-year-old daughter and I were returning home from a walk. After we entered the foyer, I turned and started to close the door. But I stopped when my daughter cried out, "Mommy, mommy, don't close the door! Cappia is coming in!" I dutifully held the door open until she assured me that her elemental friend had joined us inside.

 ## Just a Difference in Vibrations

*S*ir Arthur Conan Doyle, the brilliant creator of Sherlock Holmes, came to believe in the existence of nature spirits after much exploration and thought.

In *The Secret Life of Nature*, Peter Tompkins reports, "Doyle pointed out that in the rational world of physics we see objects only within the very limited band of frequencies that make up our color spectrum, whereas infinite vibrations, unseen by most humans, exist on either side of them."

Doyle wrote, "If we could conceive a race of

beings constructed in material which threw out shorter or longer vibrations, they would be invisible unless we could tune ourselves up, or tune them down.... If high-tension electricity can be converted by a mechanical contrivance into a lower tension, keyed to other uses, then it isn't hard to see why something analogous might not occur with the vibrations of ether and the waves of light."

> *The whole secret of the study of nature lies in learning how to use one's eyes.*
>
> – GEORGE SAND

Tompkins notes that inventors Thomas Edison and Nikola Tesla, contemporaries of Doyle, seemed to be on the same track. They both were trying to develop a device that could communicate with and photograph the spirits who peopled the fairy world.

Doyle came to the conclusion that mankind's cooperation with these nature spirits could greatly enhance the future of our civilization. "It is hard for the mind to grasp," he wrote, "what the ultimate results may be if we have actually proved the existence upon the surface of this planet of a population which may be as numerous as the human race, which pursues its own strange life in its own strange way, and which is only separated from ourselves by some difference of vibrations."

"Look, No Stockings!"

Unlike those inventors, this toddler didn't need a photograph to know how an elemental looks.

I worked in a preschool where we would read to the children from Cicely Mary Barker's flower fairy books. I would show each picture to the children and point out what was different about each fairy: this one wore a dress, that one wore shoes, another had bare feet, and so on. One day I was walking with a little toddler girl. As we passed by a potted jade plant, she stopped me, pointed to the area of the plant and said, "Look, no stockings!"

Seeing with Spiritual Vision

*M*y late husband and teacher, Mark Prophet, had the ability to see nature spirits. He once explained: "Elementals are usually not visible to mortal sight, although on rare occasions they have become so.... They are not actually invisible; they're out of the range of ordinary human sight. And therefore, you can see elementals if you know how to refocus your consciousness and your eyes and other faculties that you have that are spiritual in nature."

Paradise Lost?

In past golden ages, angels, elementals and humanity worked in complete harmony. Mark Prophet once gave us a glimpse of that world when he described what the earth could look like if the elementals were not bowed down with mental, emotional and physical pollution.

If we had followed the divine plan, we would be able to see and be friends with the nature spirits. We would not have to deal with lesser or greater storms. The ground would shed forth dew to water our crops. No rain would fall, but a dew would appear from the air.

The air would be saturated with moisture in just the right amounts everywhere on earth, and the deserts would bloom as the rose. There would be no excess moisture and no lack of it; it would be just right for every climate. You would have the most beautiful weather and ... the most beautiful flowers all over the world.

You would have plenty of food and ... there would be abundant fruit. Many of the fruits that would manifest are not even on the planet now.... We would have communion with the elementals, and we would be receiving our instructions from angels.

Reflections

1. Mankind's thoughts, words and deeds—both posi-
    tive and negative—affect the environment, nature
    and weather patterns. In what ways do you see
    this occurring?

2. Can you remember a time when you were in
    nature and felt more than just the physical
    presence of the natural elements? What was
    this like for you?

3. How do you feel now about spending time in
    nature? In what ways are your thoughts and
    feelings changing?

PART 2

Nature's Inner Workings

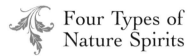

Four Types of Nature Spirits

There are four types of nature spirits—gnomes, sylphs, salamanders and undines—and they sustain the elements of earth, air, fire and water. Day after day, they work to purify these elements and to keep the earth on an even keel. They regulate all the natural processes on the planet.

Those who have probed the world of the elementals tell us that they are by nature joyous, carefree, innocent, loyal and trusting, and in past ages they served in harmony with mankind. But there came a time when mankind's negativity was introduced into their world, and their job got much harder. They now had to function in a denser world and restore balance where there was increasing imbalance.

For centuries and millennia, the burden of mankind's negative thoughts, words and deeds has been building up. The elementals have been carrying

For I have learned to look on nature, not as in the hour of thoughtless youth, but hearing often-times the still, sad music of humanity.

— WILLIAM WORDSWORTH

this weight and trying to regain planetary equilibrium.

I believe it will take the renewed cooperation between men and elementals to restore the ecology of earth's biosphere to proper balance. To understand how we can accomplish this, we'll take a closer look at the four groups of nature spirits and what they do for us.

Tending the Earth Element

The nature spirits who serve at the physical level are called gnomes. Billions of gnomes tend the earth through the cycles of the four seasons and see to it that all living things are supplied with their daily needs. They also process the waste and by-products that are an inevitable part of our everyday existence.

The gnomes do everything to tend and care for the earth element. They're responsible for enriching the soil and for the formation of all the minerals and elements found in the earth. They also protect and maintain the form and texture of the flowers,

> *Fieldes have eies and woods have eares.*
>
> – JOHN HEYWOOD,
> 16TH CENTURY POET

leaves, stalks, plants—everything that is produced in the earth. Mark Prophet once said, "I have become aware that every single manifestation in nature is presided over by elementals—that there is no flower growing anywhere, not even a blade of grass, that does not have an elemental presiding over it."

Rose Bushes Rescued

One woman wrote to me about how the elementals saved her precious flowers.

The beautiful rose bushes in my garden were under attack. Aphids were infesting all of the leaves on every rose bush. So I asked the elementals, "If you would be so kind as to get

*some ladybugs to take care of the aphids,
I would be very grateful." The next morning
when I came out to check the garden, I saw
ladybugs on all of the roses and the aphids
were gone. I thanked the elementals.*

Those who have the gift of inner vision and can see beyond the physical realm have described what the nature spirits look like. The gnomes, they say, are often short and impish, but not always. They can appear as three-inch-high elves playing in the grasses to three-foot-high dwarfs to giant-sized gnomes.

In addition to maintaining the cycles of growth in the earth, the hardworking gnomes purge the earth of poisons and pollutants that are dangerous to the physical bodies of man, animal and plant life—including toxic wastes, industrial effluvia, pesticides, acid rain, nuclear radiation and every abuse of the earth.

On spiritual levels, the gnomes have an even heavier chore. They must clean up the imprints of mankind's discord and negativity that remain at energetic levels in the earth. War, murder, rape, child abuse, the senseless killing and torture of animals, profit seeking at the expense of the environment as well as hatred, anger, discord, gossip—all these create an accumulation of negatively charged energy that becomes a weight on the earth body and on the nature spirits.

Like the tides of the sea and the currents of the air, all energy moves in rhythmic flow. Patterns of energy-flow between and among people, whether harmful or benign, must sooner or later recycle through the planet. And in the process, these patterns are assimilated and outplayed by the forces of nature.

> *We cannot remember too often that when we observe nature…, it is always ourselves alone we are observing.*
> — GEORG CHRISTOPH LICHTENBERG, 18TH CENTURY PHYSICIST

Nurturing the Water Element

The nature spirits whose domain is the water element are known as undines. These beautiful, supple mermaidlike beings are subtle and swift in their movements and can change form rapidly.

The sea has many life-sustaining functions supported by the undines, who maintain the wondrous gardens of the seas. These elementals govern water and its energies wherever they are, not only large bodies of water but also smaller sources.

The undines control all of the fish and mineral life in the seas and in the waters of the earth. They also control the tides and have much to do with the

> *To me, the sea is like a person—like a child that I've known a long time. It sounds crazy, I know, but when I swim in the sea I talk to it. I never feel alone when I'm out there.*
>
> — GERTRUDE EDERLE*

*Olympic Gold Medalist and the first woman to swim across the English Channel.

climate as well as oxygenation and precipitation. Since three-fourths of the surface of the earth is covered with water, the undines are quite busy!

They work on the purification of water everywhere, even in the body of man. Their job is to cleanse the waters of the planet that have been poisoned by sewage, oil spills, industrial waste, chemicals, pesticides and other substances. They toil ceaselessly to heal the polluted seas as they recharge the electromagnetic field of the waters with currents of the Spirit. Their bodies are conductors of cosmic currents resounding through the chambers of submarine life.

The undines cleanse not only the physical waters but also that aspect of mankind's life that relates to the water element, their emotions. Emotion can be described as "energy in motion." Like water, it has tremendous power and movement. Also like water, emotions can suddenly come upon us and easily move us in or out of a balanced perspective.

The undines carry the weight of mankind's emotional pollution—feelings that are not at peace, such as anger, fear and anxiety.

 ## Directing the Air Element

The next group of nature spirits is the sylphs, and they tend the air element, directing the flow of air currents and atmospheric conditions. They purify the atmosphere and aerate every cell of life with the sacred breath of Spirit. They are bearers of *prana,* or breath of life, which nourishes all living things. On subtle levels, the sylphs transmit the currents of the Spirit from heaven to the atmosphere of earth.

The sylphs often have thin, ethereal bodies that transform gracefully into myriad shapes as they soar through the air. The trackless realms of the air are their domain, and their trackings are often defined by the formation and reformation of the clouds. Sylphs are able to travel at great distances quickly, and giant sylphs can span the skies and interpenetrate the earth,

the water and the fire elements.

The Blue Eyes of a Sylph

On a stormy night, this traveler had a surprise visit from a sylph.

I was a passenger on a Boeing 747 flying to Los Angeles. It was a stormy night and we were tossed around like a piece of paper. The wind and turbulence were terrible, and the lightning lit the darkened cabin like day. There were very few people on that plane, so I scurried to a window away from everyone and said some intense prayers. To hide the sound of my voice, I pressed my face against the glass near one of the jets. With my eyes squeezed shut, I implored heaven and the elementals to save us.

I paused, took a deep breath and opened my eyes. Suddenly, I was looking right into the incredible blue eyes of a sylph! It took me a second to realize that the sylph was on the outside of the glass. It really shocked me! But finally I was able to speak and I said, "You're outside!"

The sylph answered, "Yes, and we will take care of you. Do not be afraid."

Soon afterwards the plane was flying above the storm, and all was peaceable.

If we want to get a closer look at the sylphs, we can see them through the eyes of Mark Prophet. "These are the types of elementals you see with long hair and rather thin, seraphiclike bodies, and they're very curvaceous. They float through the air and they'll bend their whole body in different shapes. Sometimes the body is bent with the legs behind, trailing like a garment, and their arms are in the most graceful ballerina poses.

"They have beautiful faces, like the most beautiful woman imaginable, except that they're soul faces." The only exceptions, Mark said, are when they take on a human form reflecting negative human attitudes.

Like giant transformers, sylphs conduct the currents of the mind of God to the mind of man. They also work to purify the air of pollutants—everything from car exhaust and volatile organic compounds to toxic fumes emitted from factories and other industrial processes—before these can pollute the water and the earth.

The air element corresponds to the mental level of existence, or the mind, which is like the air in that its capacity is unlimited. So the sylphs also have the job of purifying the mental plane, which can become polluted by negative thoughts that feed hatred, anger, racial prejudice, religious bigotry, resentment, pride, ambition, greed, jealousy and other such poisons.

Controlling the
Fire Element

The fourth group of nature spirits work with the fire element and they're called salamanders. Their job is crucial, for they serve at the atomic level of all organic and inorganic life, infusing the molecules of matter with the spiritual fires of creation.

The garments of the salamanders appear as pulsating rainbow fires emitting the full spectrum of the rainbow rays. These fiery nature spirits are tall, majestic beings. In fact, they're the biggest, most powerful elementals of all. We can imagine their size if we think about how a large, towering fire can sweep through a forest.

The salamanders imbue the entire creation with the energies of the Spirit necessary to sustain life on earth. Capable of wielding the most intense fires of the physical atom as well as the purifying fires of Spirit, they control the spiritual-material oscillation of light within the nucleus of every atom.

Whether in electricity, firelight or the flame of

a candle, the salamanders are agents for the transfer of the fires of the subtle world for mankind's daily use. Without the spark of life sustained by the salamanders, life and matter begin to decay, corrode and disintegrate.

The burdens upon the salamanders range from the weight of mankind's hatred to irresponsible uses of nuclear energy. Were it not for the fiery salamanders absorbing and transmuting the huge conglomerates of negativity over the large cities of the world, crime and darkness would be much more advanced and rampant than they are today.

The very sustaining of life—the air we breathe, the food we eat, the water we drink—is something most of us take for granted. Yet at the most basic

level, we are utterly dependent on the selfless service of the nature spirits. The miracle of life is the miracle of the gnomes, undines, sylphs and salamanders.

Reflections

1. Reflect on the four groups of nature spirits. Which ones do you feel an affinity for and why?

2. Remember a time in your life when a circumstance in nature was alleviated or improved. Which elementals do you perceive as having been involved in helping the situation?

3. How do any movies, books or stories you've seen about nature or the elementals relate to what you've read about in this book?

PART 3

The Mirror of Man

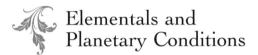

Elementals and Planetary Conditions

The elementals have a certain plasticity to their nature, an almost chameleonlike quality that causes them to take on the vibrations of their surroundings. They mimic mankind and are easily influenced by our thoughts and feelings, both positive and negative. Their mimicry of our discord, generated currently as well as in the past, can cause raging floodwaters, biting winds, angry storms and searing heat.

So in a very real way, the outer turbulence we see in the elements is a reflection of what's taking place within mankind. Mark Prophet explained, for example, that "when the sylphs take on negative human attitudes and qualities of discord, they will desire to rid themselves of these. They will throw off the human vibrations of hatred and anger by starting a whirling action in the air. They can whirl so fast that they can develop winds of a hundred and fifty miles an hour, which is the power

> *Nature always tends to act in the simplest way.*
>
> – BERNOULLI,
> 18TH CENTURY MATHEMATICIAN

behind the hurricane."

But the nature spirits don't only mimic and take on humanity's vibrations. They also become supersaturated with the planetary momentum of negative elements at the physical, mental and emotional levels.

When the burden becomes too heavy, they become tired and listless, just as we do when we're overworked. And when they're no longer able to bear that burden, they're forced to literally convulse and shrug off the heavy weight. This can result in earthquakes, floods, tornadoes, hurricanes and, as a last resort, large-scale cataclysm. I believe that is exactly what happened when Pompeii was buried under volcanic cinders and ash.

It's similar to what we ourselves may have experienced or observed in other people. For instance, someone you love comes home and all of a sudden erupts like a volcano or explodes in a tirade. It's unexpected, and yet it has probably been building for a long time. That person has been carrying some burden, even if it has been invisible to you. It's like an internal volcano. And the longer he or she has carried it, the more steam it has gathered. This is what happens to elemental life.

Therefore it's not so much that Mother Nature is "mad" but that she is sad and weary. She is burdened. And like a mirror, she is reflecting back to us our own madness, our own craziness, because that is the only way she can get our attention. It's the only way she can shake us awake before it's too late.

No man, no woman is an island; we are all interconnected. When we blow our tops or, against our better judgment, engage in gossip or criticism, we add to the planetary momentum of negative elements that weigh down the nature spirits.

> *Humankind has not woven the web of life. We are but one thread within it. Whatever we do to the web, we do to ourselves. All things are bound together.*
>
> – ATTRIBUTED TO CHIEF SEATTLE*

---

*English rendition inspired by Chief Seattle's prophetic speech, which he gave upon hearing the terms of a proposed treaty that would take his people's land from them.

The negative energy we put out attracts more of its kind. Unless we seek and find resolution, that energy will, by the law of karma, return to us. And once it becomes physical, there is little we can do about it.

 Caring for Our Planet

The imbalance in our ecosystem is significant and serious, which doesn't portend well for holding back physical ramifications. However, if we care for our planet, for every species on it and for all elemental life, we can eventually restore balance. How can we care for the nature spirits and relieve their plight? What can we do to make peace with Mother Nature?

Given the weight of world karma and the high levels of pollution and ecological imbalance in many parts of the earth, it is a daunting task. But it is not impossible. We have the material and spiritual tools we need to do the job.

On a physical level, we as individuals and nations of course need to move quickly to clean up all
kinds of existing pollution and prevent creating
more. We can each do our part by making choices
that promote greater health and harmony for ourselves, future generations and our planet. It can be,
for example, by recycling, buying organic produce,
reducing emissions, minimizing consumption of
natural resources. Some individuals may bring
forth new technologies, inventions or products
that address existing problems and prevent future
ones from occurring. Whatever we do, it will take
unprecedented cooperation and the mobilizing of
inner and outer resources to bring the scales back
into balance.

 Reverence for Life

*O*n a personal level, we can take responsibility to master our own negatives, including
habits that may harm ourselves and others and

contribute to the mental, emotional and physical pollution of the earth.

We can consciously give gratitude to the invisible workers behind the visible wonders of nature, whether it's in the blessing we offer before we eat our meals or the prayer we whisper before we lay our heads down at night. For without the unflagging work of the elementals, we would not have a physical platform to live on. We would not have a place to work out our karma or to grow spiritually.

We can remind ourselves and each other to honor and respect nature, the material world and our physical surroundings as chalices for the Spirit. For, as Albert Schweitzer once said, "If a man loses his reverence for any part of life, he will soon lose his reverence for all of life."

> *People have got to understand that the commandment "Do unto others as you would that they should do unto you" applies to animals, plants and things, as well as to people!*
>
> – ALDOUS HUXLEY

Empowerment through the Divine Spark

The situation on earth is so critical that it impels us to turn to God and resolve to be humble before the awesome influences we've unleashed on this planet. For man cannot control the environment or forestall catastrophes like the ones we're seeing today, and have seen down through the ages, except through spiritual means. We need God when we're in the midst of solving such problems. God and the essence of God within us, the spiritual flame in our hearts, is the best hope we have for solving any problem.

Beginning with the microcosm of self, we are empowered by God through the divine spark within to take control of our environment and our lives. And by taking more responsibility for what is happening to our children and our people, by being wise stewards of our planet, we can shake off our complacency—and thereby perhaps avoid the need to be shaken awake by nature.

Just as important as our actions to restore

balance on the physical, mental and emotional levels is our spiritual work. And this can be most effective if we are aware of our own spiritual re-source, our own divine identity. Indeed, this is the foundation of our work with the elementals. By knowing who we truly are, our Higher Self, we can access the light and power that can help us join with the elementals to clean up pollution, restore balance to our ecosystem, and mitigate or trans-mute the karma that already is everywhere spilling over into the physical.

Our Divine Identity

The Chart of Your Divine Self illustrates your vast spiritual potential and destiny. It is a portrait of you and God within you. The upper figure is your "I AM Presence," the Presence of God that is individualized for each of us.

The middle figure represents your Higher Self—your inner teacher, voice of conscience and dearest friend. Jesus discovered the Higher Self to be "the Christ" and Gautama discovered it to be "the Buddha." Thus, the Higher Self is sometimes called the Inner Christ (or Christ Self) or the Inner

THE CHART OF YOUR DIVINE SELF

Buddha. Christian mystics sometimes refer to it as the inner man of the heart or the Inner Light. And the Upanishads mysteriously describe it as a being the "size of a thumb" who "dwells deep within the heart." Whether we call it the Christ, the Buddha, the Atman or the Tao, each of us is meant to become one with our Higher Self.

The lower figure represents you on the spiritual path, surrounded by the protective white light of God and the violet flame. (See pages 101–10 for more on the violet flame.) Surrounding the I AM Presence are seven concentric spheres of light that make up what is called the causal body. Each sphere denotes a different aspect, or quality, of cosmic consciousness that you have developed throughout your lifetimes. These qualities manifest as talents and genius. All of us have a unique causal body from which we can draw down our individual gifts.

The ribbon of white light descending from the heart of the I AM Presence through the Higher Self to the lower figure is the crystal cord. It is the umbilical cord, or lifeline, that ties you to Spirit.

This stream of spiritual energy nourishes and sustains the flame of God within your heart, which is your soul's potential to be one with God.

God has so loved us that he has placed this flame within us as a portion of himself to which we have recourse. This divine spark is our point of contact with God.

"By This Name I Shall Be Invoked"

God told Moses to tell the children of Israel that his name was I AM THAT I AM and that "I AM hath sent me unto you." Moreover, he said, "This is my name for ever, and this is my memorial unto all generations." The Jerusalem Bible translates the last sentence: "This is my name for all time; by this name I shall be invoked for all generations to come."

When we call upon the name of the Lord, as the prophets tell us to do, we use the name I AM THAT I AM or simply I AM. So to address the God Presence—which is universal and individual—we say, "Beloved mighty I AM Presence . . ."

Your Protective Tube of Light

The tube of light, shown in the Chart of Your Divine Self, is a cylinder of energy about nine feet in diameter that can protect you from negative energy and even from physical danger. It descends from the I AM Presence above you and extends beneath your feet.

When you are in difficult situations, including severe climatic changes, you need to remain calm. You may feel fear, confusion, helplessness—from within yourself or from other people. The tube of light can help you to stay centered and at peace.

The tube of light also guards you from negative energies that may be directed at you through another person's anger, condemnation, hatred or jealousy. When you are unprotected, these vibrations can make you irritable or depressed and can even cause mishaps.

To establish a protective light around yourself, give the "Tube of Light" affirmation three times with devotion. It is helpful to do this before you begin your day.

Tube of Light

Beloved I AM Presence bright,
Round me seal your tube of light
From ascended master flame
Called forth now in God's own name.
Let it keep my temple free
From all discord sent to me.

I AM calling forth violet fire
To blaze and transmute all desire,
Keeping on in freedom's name
Till I AM one with the violet flame.

As you recite this affirmation, see yourself as depicted in the Chart of Your Divine Self. Your Higher Self is above you. Above your Higher Self is your I AM Presence, the Presence of God with you.

See and feel a waterfall of dazzling white light, brighter than the sun shining on new-fallen snow, tumbling down from your I AM Presence to envelop you. See it coalescing to form an impenetrable wall of light.

Inside that scintillating aura of white light,

see yourself surrounded with the violet flame, a powerful high-frequency spiritual energy that transforms negativity, your own or another's, into positive and loving energy.

From time to time throughout the day, reinforce this spiritual protection by repeating the tube of light prayer and visualizing yourself enfolded in a tube of brilliant white light.

The Violet Flame

You can access the transforming energy of the violet flame by giving a mantra, a short spoken prayer consisting of a repeated word or group of words. It invokes a particular aspect or quality of the Divinity, intensifying the action of God's Spirit in man.

Try repeating the following mantra as you go about your day. When you recite this and other mantras which invoke the violet flame, that flame permeates every cell and atom of your body. It penetrates into your mind, your emotions, your subconscious and your memory. The more often you repeat these prayers, the greater the momentum of violet flame you can build.

> I AM a being of violet fire!
> I AM the purity God desires!

Using this short mantra, you can give a quick, powerful call for action in all types of circumstances.

And so, using the name of God, I AM THAT I AM, we can call forth our tube of light and violet flame to fortify us as we work with the elementals.

Reflections

1. What are two practical things that you can do in your local community to help the nature spirits?

2. What can you do spiritually, through your Higher Self and the violet flame, to help the elementals and promote planetary equilibrium?

3. What are your reflections about your divine identity?

4. When you observe Mother Nature being "angry"—
    a hurricane, tornado, wildfire, earthquake or flash
    flood—pause to think about what kinds of feelings
    or energy these conditions might be reflecting.
    Have you felt anything similar through another
    person or group of people, or seen it on television?
    Have you ever felt that way yourself?

PART 4

Developing a Dynamic Relationship with the Elementals

Commanding the
Elementals

*J*esus had command over the forces of nature. When he said, "Peace, be still," it was done— the wind and waves immediately ceased their troubled activity.

Mark Prophet also had mastery in working with the elementals. One summer while Mark and I lived in Colorado Springs, we had a hailstorm that was damaging the plants in our garden. So Mark and I went to our chapel to pray about it, and Mark made the command to the elementals to stop the hail. He said something to the effect, "In the name of my God Presence, I command the beings of the air, earth, water and fire to cease this hail. Let it cease this instant in the name of the living God."

The elementals didn't pay any attention to him at all. It kept right on hailing. So Mark raised his voice, and his voice took on the power and authority of God—you could feel the fire crackle. He repeated the same command with power, and the hail stopped instantly.

The key to dominion in the earth is oneness with God. You cannot do anything outside of God. You cannot command his energies if you have spiritual pride in your accomplishments, if you look down on other parts of life, if you think that you are somehow outside of the sphere of God's consciousness.

Mark Prophet had the awareness, a living awareness, of his oneness with God. With this consciousness and conviction, he could command the elementals as the instrument of God's power. And with this consciousness, we too can invoke the power of God to command the elementals.

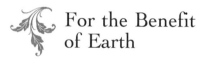 For the Benefit of Earth

Regarding how to command the elementals, I counsel all to use these teachings wisely and responsibly for the benefit of mankind and the earth. I have come across people who have manipulated elemental life for their own convenience or whim, sometimes causing great and lasting harm. Mark Prophet spoke of this as a "gross misuse of power," even though sometimes "people don't know what they're doing."

But we have a safeguard. It is by obedience to the laws of God and by love, Mark said, that we are able to help the elementals and our planet. With this, if our motivation is pure, then our

> *Send forth intense love, appreciation, compassion and the wisdom of the law to the mighty salamanders.... They are obedient unto those who are obedient unto the law of love.*
>
> – HIERARCHS OF THE FIRE ELEMENT

work with the elementals can be constructive. And part of our pure motive is the desire to do what's right and to please God. "If we want to do it to please God," Mark said, "he knows that."

The Secret Is Love

Understanding the Language of Nature

*L*uther Burbank was known during his lifetime as one of America's foremost horticulturists. Burbank developed more than eight hundred new varieties of plants and had a great attunement with nature.

After a visit to Burbank, Helen Keller wrote in Outlook for the Blind: "He has the rarest of gifts, the receptive spirit of a child. When plants talk to him, he listens. Only a wise child can understand the language of flowers and trees."

The Hindu saint Yogananda also commented on a meeting he had with Burbank:

"'The secret of improved plant breeding, apart from scientific knowledge, is love.' Luther Burbank uttered this wisdom as I walked beside him in his garden

*in Santa Rosa, California. We halted near
a bed of edible cacti.*

*"'While I was conducting experiments
to make "spineless" cacti,' he continued,
'I often talked to the plants to create a
vibration of love. You have nothing to
fear, I would tell them. You don't need
your defensive thorns. I will protect you.
Gradually the useful plant of the desert
emerged in a thornless variety.'"*

In the 1906 San Francisco earthquake, almost every building in nearby Santa Rosa was destroyed. Notably, Burbank's house was undamaged and not a single pane of glass in his greenhouse was broken. While others described this as a miracle, Burbank considered it to be the work of the forces of nature, who did not wish to see his experiments interrupted.

Brothers and Sisters in Nature

Francis of Assisi, one of the most beloved saints of all time, celebrated life in his great love for all of nature. He was born into a well-to-do merchant family around 1181 or 1182 in the town of Assisi, Italy. As a young man, Francis had a world-liness and zest for life that made him a favorite among his companions. Then, during his twenties, he embraced a life of poverty, serving the sick and preaching. His simple, sincere message touched *people deep inside their hearts.*

Artists often depict Francis surrounded by birds and other animals. For he saw the presence of God in nature and had a great love and respect for all creatures. All created things, he said, are our brothers and sisters because we all have the same Father.

Early stories say that when Francis preached, the birds would surround him and remain still until he finished his sermon. Other creatures were drawn to him as well, and he cared for them and encouraged others to do so. Francis is said to have delighted in communing with "wildflowers, the crystal spring, and the friendly fire," and in greeting the rising sun.

Francis loved to sing popular songs as well as his own improvised hymns of praise. Near the end of his life, he composed his "Canticle of the Sun" in praise of the Creator and his creation.

From "Canticle of the Sun"

*We praise you, Lord, for all your
    creatures,
Especially for Brother Sun,
Who is the day through whom you
    give us light.
And he is beautiful and radiant with
    great splendor,
Of you Most High, he bears your likeness.*

*We praise you, Lord, for Sister Moon
    and the stars.
In the heavens you have made
    them bright, precious and fair.*

*We praise you, Lord, for Brothers Wind
    and Air,
Fair and stormy, all weather's moods,
By which you cherish all that you
    have made.*

*We praise you, Lord, for Sister Water,
So useful, humble, precious and pure.*

We praise you, Lord, for Brother Fire,
Through whom you light the night.
He is beautiful, playful, robust
    and strong.

We praise you, Lord, for Sister Earth,
Who sustains us with her fruits,
    colored flowers, and herbs.

Working with the Nature Spirits

*L*earning to work with the nature spirits is like learning anything else—it takes practice. Try giving some time to this each day, even ten minutes. Offer prayers to the violet flame for them. Give them the love of your heart. Giving regularly to the nature spirits builds trust. It's a little like feeding the birds; once they learn that you're going to be there every day, that you're going to feed them, they'll keep coming back.

> *Conscious...cooperation with elemental life requires a reeducation of the heart of both God's children and the childlike elementals.*
>
> – HIERARCHS OF THE FIRE ELEMENT

When you work with the elementals, in some ways it's similar to working with children. And the more you understand children, the more you will understand the elementals. They see through people just like children do. They sense people's ulterior motives. They sense when someone is manipulating them because of pride or ambition. They serve the pure in heart, and that's why they're often around children.

You may decide to cultivate within yourself childlike qualities, like purity of heart—so that the elementals will trust you, so that by attunement with your Higher Self you can teach them and work with them for the good, for the restoration of harmony and balance to the planet.

Keys for Working with the Elementals

1. Make your request in the name of your Higher Self.

2. Command the elementals in the name of the hierarchs who guide and lead them. They are Virgo and Pelleur, who are over the gnomes, Aries and Thor over the sylphs, Oromasis and Diana over the salamanders, and Neptune and Luara over the undines. Always command them in love and in a state of attunement with your Higher Self. If you have fear, anger or any other inharmonious vibration, first do the spiritual work to center yourself.

3. Spend some time working with the elementals

every day. Develop an ongoing active relationship with them. Give them assignments.

4. Always ask for the will of God. Regardless of the situation, it is always safe to ask the archangels and the hierarchs of the elementals to take charge. And you can command the elementals to follow the directions of their hierarchs.

Try getting to know the elementals. This can be especially helpful if you have fear or anxiety about the weather or natural disasters. Get involved with them, talk with them. You can teach them how to give prayers to the violet flame. I have called to the elementals to sit down with me and I have taught them simple violet-flame decrees as I would teach children. (See pages 104–6 for an explanation of decrees.)

When you have an ongoing relationship with elemental life, when you have an established habit of calling to their hierarchs, then you are less likely to feel as though sometime, somewhere you might be involved in some type of cataclysm. Instead, you gain confidence and trust in your relationship with nature.

"Practice Makes Perfect"

*As with all things, practice makes perfect....
And your practice with elemental life—sending
forth the power of peace from the heart, giving the
command, giving love, summoning the elementals
in your service, calling to the hierarchs—will be
rewarded.*

*I assure you that it takes time for elementals,
just as for the animal kingdom who have been
affrighted by humanity, to become accustomed to
the idea that embodied sons of God will do them no
harm, will speak only the will of God....*

*And by and by, little by little, almost with a
certain timidity, you will find salamanders and
gnomes and undines and sylphs following you like
a mighty army.*

— ELOHIM OF THE FIFTH RAY

Reflections

1. It is not necessary for you to see the nature spirits to develop a relationship with them. A good way to begin cultivating this relationship is to contemplate with gratitude the air you breathe, the water you drink, the warmth of the sun, and the firmness of the earth beneath your feet. What could you do to enhance your relationship with elemental life?

2. What might you do to develop a sense of mutual trust and respect with the elementals?

PART 5

What to Do for Specific Emergencies

 Fires

Many years ago when we were in Idaho, some workers accidentally started a fire on our land while burning garbage. That summer was exceptionally dry, and the flames raced over the land like a prairie fire.

I commanded the fiery salamanders to recede so that the fire would turn back upon itself and be contained. I also gave the decree "Reverse the Tide" (see page 139). As long as I continued to give this decree, the elementals would obey and the fire would retreat. But as soon as I would stop, the fire would advance again.

From this experience, I gained a greater understanding of the character of fire elementals and commanding the forces of nature. I recognized that the elementals have a profound respect for the sons and daughters of God, for their hierarchs and other heavenly beings whom we call upon through our prayers.

And even though the elementals attempt to be obedient, sometimes they get caught up and bound in the vortexes of wind. As they are tossed and tumbled about, they can be overtaken and embroiled in winds and fires that wreak havoc. They can also become the victims of forces that intentionally manipulate them.

Because of their temperament, working with fire elementals requires a delicate understanding and balance. If they have too much freedom, they can get out of hand. But if they are too limited, they can't do their job.

Therefore, call to the Elohim* and the angels of protection to free the elementals where they need to be freed and to bring them under the God-control and direction of their hierarchs. Then surrender your calls to the will of God.

Practical Strategies for Dealing with Fires

1. Make sure that you are in a safe place.

2. Notify the fire department and take the appropriate steps for the situation.

*For more on the Elohim, see page 110.

3. Call to Archangel Michael,* the great angel of protection, and his blue-lightning angels to cut free the salamanders. Ask Michael and his angels to free these fiery elementals from the forces and burdens of negative energies and from the physical vortexes of the wind and fire.

4. Pray to the hierarchs of the fire element, Oromasis and Diana, to bring the salamanders under their control and to direct them to contain the fire.

5. Pray to the hierarchs of the air element, Aries and Thor, to bring winds from the direction that will turn the fire back upon itself.

6. Call to Archangel Michael for the protection of the firefighters as well as the lives and property of those who may be in the path of the fire.

7. For larger forest fires, find out which weather patterns would be most beneficial for fighting the fire and bringing rain. Ask the sylphs and undines to manifest those patterns and to bring rain or snow, as appropriate, to put out the fire.

8. Offer prayers and decrees for the situation,

---

*For more on Archangel Michael, see pages 135–38.

including the prayers on behalf of the elementals on pages 93–96.

9. Remember to ask for your requests to be adjusted according to the will of God.

 Hurricanes

Each year hurricanes beat against the Gulf and Atlantic coasts of North America. These storms originate as tropical disturbances in the Atlantic Ocean off the coast of Africa. Trade winds blow the storms westward across the Atlantic Ocean, and they gather more energy in the Caribbean and the Gulf of Mexico.

From a spiritual perspective, hurricanes can result from focuses of hatred produced by practitioners of voodoo and black magic in their ceremonies. Elementals who get caught in the vortexes of this misused energy create the hurricanes. When this occurs, we are not only dealing with the effect of the hurricane itself but also with tremendous forces of hatred or other negative energies.

But the misuses of energy, including focuses of hatred, are not the only cause of hurricanes and tornadoes. Another factor is the return of mankind's karma. As previously mentioned, one of the greatest ways that karma is expiated is by the elemental forces, who bear the burden of mankind's negativity. When they can no longer carry this weight, they throw it off, which often results in natural disasters and cataclysm.

Therefore, in working with violent storms and other forms of cataclysm, it is of utmost importance to call for the will of God. For we don't know if it may be necessary for mankind to experience some kind of physical return of this energy in order to work out their karma.

So we call for the will of God, and we also call for mercy. And we call for the clearing of forces of darkness. But a hurricane or another natural disaster may still occur. And if it does, we need to remember that heavenly beings cannot stand between man and his karma.

We do all that we can to safeguard and protect ourselves on physical and spiritual levels. We make the calls we know to make. And then we say, "Thy will be done."

Practical Strategies for Dealing with Hurricanes

1. If you are in a place that is directly threatened by a hurricane, make the necessary physical preparations, including evacuation if necessary. Develop a family plan so that all members understand what to do if a disaster strikes while individual members are in separate locations.

2. If you are in an area that is immediately endangered by a hurricane, your top priority is to get to safety. Then direct the elementals, their hierarchs and other heavenly beings to head it off.

3. Call to the Elohim and to Archangel Michael and the blue-lightning angels to place a blue sphere around the hurricane with its energy vortex and to redirect it to an area where it will not be destructive to life. Call to these beings to cut the sylphs and undines free from energies of hatred and black magic that have been imposed upon them.

4. Place the sylphs under the authority of their hierarchs, Aries and Thor, and the undines under their hierarchs, Neptune and Luara. Ask these hierarchs

to take command of the elementals, including those that have been imprisoned or trapped, as well as the vortex of negativity that they have been caught up in.

5. Send violet flame to the elementals to transmute the burdens of mankind's energy that they are bearing.

6. Call to Archangel Michael for the protection of the lives and property of those who may be in the path of the hurricane.

7. Offer your prayers and decrees for the situation, including the prayers on behalf of the sylphs and undines on pages 93–95.

8. Remember to ask for your requests to be adjusted according to the will of God.

A Hurricane Goes Back Out to Sea

One day Mark Prophet received a phone call from some ladies in Wilmington, North Carolina, saying that a hurricane was bearing down on the area in which they lived. The news reports were predicting a devastating hurricane that would wreak serious havoc in their area.

Mark went into action immediately and made powerful calls to God and the elemental beings. Later we heard on the news that rather than touching land, the hurricane turned completely around and went right back out to sea.

The weather bureau said that in their entire history of charting hurricanes, they had never seen anything like that! Hurricanes don't just turn around and go back out to sea. But this one did! The great love that Mark sent to the elementals soothed them enough that they could again shoulder their burdens.

Hurricane Flossie

We returned from vacation last summer to learn that Flossie, a Category Four hurricane, was churning across the Pacific toward our Big Island of Hawaii. Storm warnings were already posted, and Flossie was expected to pass within two hundred miles south of the island by the next afternoon. She was the first significant hurricane to threaten Hawaii since hurricane Iniki, also a Category Four, crashed into Kauai in 1992, leaving behind some $2.5 billion in damage.

Before we headed out to restock our batteries, bottled water and canned goods, I started my prayers and decrees for the elementals involved in the storm and for the dissipation of the storm so that there would be no damage to person or property. I also invited the elementals to decree with me. Meanwhile, we prepared for the strong winds, rain and surf that were expected.

Throughout the night and the next day, as Flossie continued on her path with 145-mph winds, I kept my vigil. As the fierce Flossie blew within 160 miles south of the island, she simply fizzled out and began to dissipate. The storm warnings were canceled, and not a drop of rain fell. The breezes were gentle and the surf calmed. A tropical storm that passed by a week earlier while we were on vacation —and not specifically praying for the elementals or the storm—had created more harm than Flossie.

Drought and Floods

*I*n many areas of the world today, we have a water crisis. Water represents and reflects mankind's emotional body, including his desires. Through an accumulation of mankind's collective wrong desiring, an imbalance in the forces of nature can be created, and it may eventually manifest as either drought or floods.

Drought is also a sign that mankind is not able to receive the pouring out of Spirit. Elemental life is in tune with Spirit, the Holy Spirit. So when there is an absence of the Spirit across the land, then there is no magnet, through the elementals, for the balance of the forces in nature.

Floods and damaging rains occur for many reasons. Like other severe climatic changes, they are one way in which a certain amount of group or planetary karma can be returned to an area. Flood conditions can represent a washing away of negative energies or forces. Other causes include a large buildup of destructive wishes and prayers of malintent that eventually spill over as a physical flood. Predictions of cataclysm can also influence events by promoting fear.

However, it is possible for conditions that cause cataclysm to be mitigated and for balance to be restored. And for this the violet flame is fundamental. People who give the violet flame with great zeal and intensity, joy and love often accomplish a great deal in their lives and experience many victories. And they may not even realize how much they have been spared by invoking this flame of the Spirit.

Each time you invoke the violet flame, you are helping to deliver yourself as well as the planet. You're helping to negate the conditions that can cause drought, flooding and other disasters. You're working with elementals who can come to the rescue and restore the balance in nature.

Practical Strategies for Dealing with Drought or Floods

1. Send your love and gratitude to the elementals and develop a working relationship with them.

2. Send the violet flame abundantly to the

elementals to transmute the energies of mankind's karma that they are bearing.

3. Send the violet flame to the people of the affected area to open their hearts to the light of the Spirit.

4. In the case of drought, find out what weather patterns will bring rain or snow to the affected area. (For example, in the northern Rockies of the United States, rain or snow could be produced by warm air bearing moisture from the Pacific Ocean meeting a cold air mass from the Arctic.) Send the thoughtform of the beneficial weather pattern to the elementals and ask them to bring it into manifestation.

5. Watch your own thoughts about the weather. We are used to thinking of sunny days as "good" and rainy days as "bad" weather. The elementals are influenced by these subconscious messages. Send them praise and gratitude when it rains, and not only for sunny days.

6. Offer your prayers and decrees for the situation, including the prayers on behalf of the undines and sylphs on pages 93–95.

7. Submit your prayers to the will of God.

Overdoing It?

The following story shows how the weather can be affected by calls to the elementals, in this case through the fervent prayers of little children.

My son and I were on the way to my mother's house in a small farming town in the Midwest. With us were my nephew and my two nieces. They decided that they wanted to have a big rainstorm so that they could play in it. Their mother was very protective and strict and didn't allow such things. But they knew that their grandma and I would think it was harmless fun.

The children asked me, "If we pray to the elementals, will they make it rain?"

I explained about God's laws and that the farmers were cutting hay and needed it dry. We couldn't ruin the hay crop just so we could play in the rain.

So they worked on the right prayer and asked the sylphs and undines, over and over, in God's name and according to his will, to just make it rain in town so as not to interfere with the crops. "And could it please be a real thunderstorm," they asked, "with lots of water?"

Just as we came close to town, out of a clear blue sky, clouds came up and poured down rain in a six-block square. It rushed into the streets in front of the house like a river! The children were ecstatic!

The thunder was horrific, and the deep water a bit frightening. My nephew said, with eyes wide, "Aunt Ellen, do you think we overdid it?"

They had a jolly time rolling in the muddy water and were very satisfied with their experiment. The freak storm was on the news and in all the papers. But the hay cutting was not affected at all!

 # Earthquakes

Scientists and seers have predicted earthquakes and other earth changes on the east and west coasts of America and elsewhere on the planet.

But violent earth changes are not necessary. With consistent use of the violet flame, we can transmute and mitigate our karma and alleviate potential violent changes. As Saint Germain has said, nature ever prefers the gentler way.

However, when elemental life can no longer keep up with mankind's growing impositions upon the earth body, sudden cataclysm and earthquakes may prove necessary. The more violet flame we invoke for ourselves and pour into the earth, the less will be the intensity of any earth changes that may occur.

My attunement with elemental life and my inner communion with God show me that when earthquakes, hurricanes, cyclones and tornadoes are karmic, the actions delivered through elemental life are scientifically precise. One house is demolished; the next house stands intact. Neither outcome is an accident; they both reflect karma. Elemental life is absolutely exact, down to the last leaf and grain of sand.

Scientists study the physical world of effects and see causes having to do with tectonic plates, the tensions in the earth's crust, and other conditions that may provide explanations for earthquakes.

But these conditions are merely the means for the outplaying of the cycles of karma.

Nevertheless, because of the violet flame, we have an opportunity day by day to arrest the spirals of impending cataclysm and reverse their predictions. For it is possible for even the most dire predictions of cataclysm to be reversed by the action of the violet flame.

Practical Strategies for Dealing with Earthquakes

1. Send the violet flame to the gnomes and into the earth to transmute the records of darkness and the burdens on the elementals.

2. Call to Archangel Michael and his legions to safeguard all elemental life and to seal them in obedience to the will of God.

3. When many people place their attention on predictions of earthquakes—whether from scientists or psychics—the projected thoughtforms from people's consciousness can cause disturbances in nature. Call for the elementals to be sealed and protected from projections of negative

thoughts and feelings, including fear.

4. Guard your thoughts and feelings. Don't let yourself get caught up in the mass consciousness or in fears of predicted earthquakes or other cataclysms.

5. Maintain your attunement with your Higher Self and the angels so that you will be receptive to their direction and find yourself out of harm's way.

6. If an earthquake has occurred, call for the comfort, healing and protection of those affected. And call for the protection of all cleanup and rescue workers. Send violet flame to clean up toxic wastes and chemicals that may have been released.

7. Call to the hierarchs of the gnomes, Virgo and Pelleur, to take dominion over these nature spirits and to direct them according to the will of God.

8. Earthquakes can cause fires, gas and water leaks, and disruptions of power and communication lines. Therefore call to the hierarchs of all the elements to take dominion over the nature spirits and the situation. Ask them to extend the maximum amount of mercy allowed by God's laws and the karma of those involved.

9. Offer your prayers and decrees for the situation, including the prayers on behalf of the elementals on pages 91–96.

10. Ask for your requests to be adjusted according to the will of God.

Reflections

1. With a positive yet practical attitude, what could you do to prepare for the specific kinds of climatic or earth changes that might occur where you live?

2. Considering the potential problems where you live, which practical strategies would you keep at hand?

3. Consider what your family plan would be in case of various natural disasters. Make sure all members understand the plan.

PART 6

Opening the Door to Heavenly Assistance

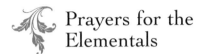

Prayers for the Elementals

Before you give your decrees, you can offer an opening prayer, or preamble, for the specific elementals for whom you are praying. You can call forth the hierarchs of these elementals as well as other heavenly beings from whom you would like help. And you can include your personal requests for the situation at hand. This will open the door to heavenly assistance and maximize the effectiveness and power of your decrees and affirmations.

Prayer on Behalf of the Gnomes

In the name of my mighty I AM Presence and my Higher Self, I ask for the energy of my prayers to be used for the upliftment of life on earth. I call to the hierarchs of the earth element, Virgo and Pelleur, to free the gnomes from the burden of man's inhumanity to man and to elemental life. Free the gnomes from the strident discord of mankind's warring—each individual's own internal warring and the warring among the peoples.

Beloved masters of the violet flame, send oceans of violet flame to clean up all pollution burdening the earth body. Clear all industrial effluvia and all toxic and nuclear wastes.

I call for the enforcement of proper waste disposal in all industries, including automobile manufacturing, chemical processing and manufacturing, electrical utilities, electronics; forest products, health care products, metal fabrication, oil and petroleum, pharmaceuticals and printing.

Quicken mankind with the wisdom and understanding to live in harmony with the earth. Release to us the inventions that are needed to restore balance and maintain our planet as a vibrant, abundant ecosystem. According to the will of God, let it be done.

Prayer on Behalf of the Sylphs

In the name of my mighty I AM Presence and my Higher Self, I call for the pure energy of the sun to cleanse the atmosphere and every cell of life. Intensify the energy of the Spirit that is the very life breath of the soul. Let it heal the sylphs and all life on earth. Let the air become the distilled pristine consciousness of the sylphs.

Violet-flame angels, clear all pollution of the air in the major cities and other areas of the world before it can pollute the water and the earth. Charge the air throughout the planet with the purifying essence of the violet flame.

Beloved hierarchs of the air element, Aries and Thor, take dominion now over all of the sylphs. Beloved heavenly hosts, release to mankind the inventions necessary to purify the air of all harmful substances, including automobile exhaust and toxic fumes as well as emissions from factories and other industrial processes. Inspire mankind with the wisdom and understanding to use clean energy sources and technology.

I call for the freeing of all sylphs (who mimic mankind's thoughts and mental images) from hate and its creations. Free the sylphs from these forcefields before they are outpictured in violent storms, cyclones and tornadoes. According to the will of God, let it be done.

Prayer on Behalf of the Undines

In the name of my mighty I AM Presence and my Higher Self, I call to the hierarchs of the water element, Neptune and Luara, to take command over the undines. I call to the legions of violet-flame angels to purify the collective unconscious of mankind. Transmute all that pollutes the emotional bodies of humanity and the waters of planet Earth.

Restore the natural flow of Spirit's fire to the seas. Lighten the weight of mankind's negative emotions borne by the undines. Protect the precious whales so that they may continue to transmit cosmic light and cosmic rays to all life on earth.

Pour out the violet flame to clean up all effluents from factories, refineries and waste treatment plants; all noneffluent industrial wastes, fertilizers, pesticides and oil; all gaseous emissions from cars and factories that pollute the waters when they are brought to earth by rain.

Restore all river and lake ecosystems to balance so that they can once more support full biological diversity. Reverse the damage to forests that has been caused by deforestation and acid rain. Purify the drinking water of earth to maintain the balance of the water element in the bodies of mankind. According to the will of God, let it be done.

Prayer on Behalf of the Salamanders

In the name of my mighty I AM Presence and my Higher Self, I call forth the violet flame to consume all radioactive substances that have burdened the salamanders and the earth through irresponsible uses of nuclear energy.

I call to Archangel Michael and your legions of blue-flame angels to free the fiery salamanders and all elementals from manipulation by those who practice the dark arts. Free the elementals from vortexes of negative energy in which they have become trapped.

I call to the hierarchs of the fire element, Oromasis and Diana, to take command of the fiery salamanders and contain all uncontrolled, destructive fires. In the name of my I AM Presence and Higher Self, I command the elementals to bring such fires under God-control.

And I ask that the salamanders be repolarized and realigned with God's holy will. According to the will of God, let it be done.

Prayer on Behalf of All Elementals

In the name of my mighty I AM Presence and my Higher Self, I call for the transmutation of all burdens upon elemental life due to the human discord and selfishness that manifests at every level of being.

I call to the Elohim to give to every elemental the divine image and vision of the golden age to come so that every elemental can hold the pattern for perfect form on earth. Let the earth be sealed in the pattern of perfection and the healing thoughtform. According to the will of God, let it be done.

Charge the Violet Flame into the Four Elements

In the name of the I AM THAT I AM, I call forth the intense action of the violet transmuting flame around every salamander, sylph, undine and gnome. Saturate the four elements—fire, air, water and earth—with the violet flame this day.

Consume the cause and core of mankind's karma that is a burden upon the nature spirits. Transmute the poisons and toxins—at physical, emotional, mental and etheric levels—that pollute our earth.

Charge the violet flame into the earth, into the waters, into the atmosphere, and into the very nucleus of fire in every atom of life. Let it be done according to God's holy will.

Heal Millions of Elementals

In the name of my mighty I AM Presence and my Higher Self and by the love, wisdom and power of the flame within my heart, I call forth the action of transmutation by the fire of my being, multiplied by the violet flame. I call forth this action on behalf of all elemental life.

I call for that portion of the flame I invoke and all that I AM to go forth now to heal millions upon millions of elementals in the earth! I dedicate my lifestream to the liberation of all elemental life. And I accept it done this hour in full power according to the will of God. Amen.

Reflections

1. Think about a situation for which you might give prayers to the nature spirits. It may be a specific climatic problem in your local area or perhaps an extreme weather pattern on the other side of your country or the world. You may want to create your own prayer for the elementals involved.

2. How could you find some time each day to pray for the nature spirits and the earth?

PART 7

The Key to Mitigating Karma

The Violet Flame

The violet flame is one of the most effective means we can use to help relieve the burdens of the nature spirits. For acting on microcosmic and macrocosmic levels, it is the great key to individual and planetary transmutation.

Just as a ray of sunlight passing through a prism is refracted into the seven colors of the rainbow, so spiritual light manifests as seven rays. Each ray has a specific color, frequency and quality of God's consciousness.

The violet flame is the seventh ray. When you invoke it in the name of God with a prayer or decree, it descends as spiritual energy charged with the qualities of mercy, forgiveness, justice, joy, freedom and transmutation.

As you begin to use the violet flame, you will experience feelings of joy, lightness, hope and newness of life, as though clouds of depression were being dissolved by the very sun of your own being....

The violet flame forgives as it frees, consumes as it transmutes, clears the records of past karma (thus balancing your debts to life), equalizes the flow of energy between yourself and other lifestreams, and propels you into the arms of the living God.

— EL MORYA KHAN

 ## Transmuting Personal and Planetary Karma

When the karma of a large group returns en masse, it can have large-scale consequences, such as changes in climatic conditions, extreme weather patterns, cataclysm and earth changes. Through these periodic disturbances in nature, the balance of the four elements is restored and the planet is purged, purified and realigned.

But these karmic returns can be disastrous.

Therefore it's preferable for the karma to be transmuted before it becomes physical. The violet flame can mitigate or transmute the buildup of mankind's karma before it reaches the physical plane. And as you work with the violet flame to transmute group karma, you can also transmute your own personal karma. As the master Saint Germain says:

"Every day as percentages of karma pass through the violet flame and you ratify that transmutation by good deeds, words and works of love and service, you are lightening the load and therefore rising to new planes of realization, new associations.... The less karma you have, the greater your opportunity day by day."

So decrees to the violet flame can transmute and soften our current karmic burdens as well as the accumulation of past karma. In fact, the violet flame can transmute any negative energy in our personal world, and it can produce positive change personally and in all areas of human life. As personal karma and planetary karma are transmuted, the burdens upon the elementals become lighter, and they can more easily maintain the balance on earth without cataclysmic changes.

The Power of the Spoken Word

*D*ecrees are powerful prayers spoken aloud in a dynamic, rhythmic manner. They're carefully worded formulas, positive statements that use the name of God, I AM THAT I AM. When we decree, we're commanding the flow of energy from Spirit to matter for personal and planetary transformation. We're not just asking for help; we're entering into a dynamic interactive partnership with our Father-Mother God.

A key to the power of decrees and mantras is to endow them with devotion. Giving decrees with love can change our world and the world around us. Devotion draws forth the presence of angels and other heavenly beings, and it opens the door to higher spiritual realms.

When we decree, we call to God by naming our I AM Presence and our Higher Self. In this way, we tap into our full God-potential.

Before you begin a decree, offer a personal

prayer asking for the specific assistance you need. Invite the elementals to decree with you and to help you cleanse your aura as well as the planet with the violet flame. Conclude by submitting your prayers to the will of God.

The body of a decree can be repeated as many times as you want in order to increase its effectiveness. The more times you give a decree, the more light you draw down into the situation you're praying about.

Whenever you make the call to the violet flame, instantaneously it begins breaking down the particles of dense substance within you—substance that has filled even the spaces between the electrons and nuclei of the atoms. It renews your mind and body. It renews your soul, polishing the jewel of consciousness.

When people use the violet flame, they often notice a tangible spiritual and physical difference. Therefore the best way for you to understand the violet flame is to experience it for yourself by giving a violet-flame decree.

Violet-Flame Decrees and Mantras

After giving your own personal prayer or one or more of the preambles in the previous chapter, you can use any one or as many of the violet-flame decrees below as you choose. It's helpful to repeat each decree or mantra three times or in multiples of three.

Radiant Spiral Violet Flame

In the name of the beloved Presence of God, I AM in me, my Higher Self, and all elemental life—fire, air, water and earth—I decree for ___[offer your personal prayer here]___. And I accept it done according to the will of God.

Radiant spiral violet flame
  Descend, now blaze through me!
Radiant spiral violet flame,
  Set free, set free, set free!

Radiant violet flame, O come,
   Expand and blaze thy light through me!
Radiant violet flame, O come,
   Reveal God's power for all to see!
Radiant violet flame, O come,
   Awake the earth and set it free!

Radiance of the violet flame,
   Expand and blaze through me!
Radiance of the violet flame,
   Expand for all to see!
Radiance of the violet flame,
   Establish mercy's outpost here!
Radiance of the violet flame,
   Come, transmute now all fear!

Violet Flame Is...

Breath of God inside each cell
    I AM the violet flame
Pulsing out the cosmic time
    I AM the violet flame
Energizing mind and heart
    I AM the violet flame
Sustaining God's creation now
    I AM the violet flame

    With all love
    With all love
    With all love

Shimmering in a crystal cave
    I AM the violet flame
Searching out all hidden pain
    I AM the violet flame
Consuming cause and core of fear
    I AM the violet flame
Revealing now the inner name
    I AM the violet flame

With all peace
With all peace
With all peace

Flashing like a lightning bolt
   I AM the violet flame
Stretching through the galaxies
   I AM the violet flame
Connecting soul and Spirit now
   I AM the violet flame
Raising you to cosmic heights
   I AM the violet flame

With all power
With all power
With all power

Accessing the Light of Heavenly Beings

When we're invoking divine assistance, we have access to innumerable heavenly beings to whom we can call. In addition to the angels, spiritual masters and the hierarchs of the elementals, there are powerful beings called Elohim. Elohim are the builders of form. So this particular Hebrew name of God, Elohim, is used in the first verse of the Bible: "In the beginning God [Elohim] created the heaven and the earth."

Elohim is a uni-plural noun referring to the masculine and feminine aspects of God. When speaking of either half, the plural form is retained because of the understanding that each half of the Divine Whole contains and is the androgynous Divine Self.

The names of the Elohim are words that are keyed to their vibration and presence. Arcturus and Victoria are the manifestation of the spiritual energy, or light, of God that is the violet ray. So giving their decree unlocks the energy and consciousness of the violet flame personified in the mighty beings Arcturus and Victoria.

You can give this decree to saturate the nature kingdom and Mother Earth with the violet transmuting flame. It will lighten their load and brighten your aura.

Arcturus, Blessed Being Bright

Beloved Presence of God, I AM in me, beloved Elohim Arcturus and Victoria, elemental life—fire, air, water and earth! I call for the transmutation of all nuclear waste, all toxic chemicals, all poisons and toxins in the environment and in the food that we eat. I call for the bathing of elemental life in the violet flame and for the holding of the balance within the earth to avert all cataclysmic activity. I call for a planetary action of the violet flame to lighten the burden of all elemental life. And I accept it done according to the will of God.

1. O Arcturus, blessed being bright,
    Flood, flood, flood our world with light;
    Bring forth perfection everywhere,
    Hear, O hear our earnest prayer.

Refrain:* Charge us with thy violet flame,
    Charge, O charge us in God's name;
    Anchor in us all secure,
    Cosmic radiance, make us pure.

---

*Give the refrain once after each verse.

2. O Arcturus, blessed Elohim,
    Let thy light all through us stream;
    Complement our souls with love
    From thy stronghold up above.

3. O Arcturus, violet flame's great master,
    Keep us safe from all disaster;
    Secure us in the cosmic stream,
    Help expand God's loving dream.

4. O Arcturus, dearest lord of might,
    By thy star radiance beaming bright,
    Fill us with thy cosmic light,
    Raise, O raise us to thy height.

And in full faith I consciously accept this manifest, manifest, manifest! (3x)* right here and now with full power, eternally sustained, all-powerfully active, ever expanding and world enfolding until all are wholly ascended in the light and free! Beloved I AM! Beloved I AM! Beloved I AM!

---

*When you see "(3x)" in decrees, it means to repeat the line or phrase three times.

"And in full faith..." is a formal closing prayer that seals the action of precipitation and causes the light from Spirit to descend tangibly into matter.

Mantras

I AM a being of violet fire!
I AM the purity God desires!

My heart is alive with violet fire!
My heart is the purity God desires!

My family is enfolded in violet fire!
My family is the purity God desires!

Earth is a planet of violet fire!
Earth is the purity God desires!

The elementals are beings of violet fire!
The elementals are the purity God desires!

I AM, I AM, I AM the resurrection and the life
of all elementals—fire, air, water and earth!

Elemental Decrees and Song

O Violet Flame, Come, Violet Flame

O violet flame, come, violet flame,
Now blaze and blaze and blaze!
O violet flame, come, violet flame,
To raise and raise and raise!

[Repeat verse between the following endings:]

1. The earth and all thereon (3x)
2. The plants and elemental creatures (3x)
3. The air, the sea, the land (3x)
4. I AM, I AM, I AM the fullness of God's
   plan fulfilled right now and forever (3x)

Set the Elementals Free

Seal, seal, seal in an ovoid bright
Of the violet fire's clear light
Every elemental, set and keep them free
From all human discord instantly.

[Repeat verse between the following endings:]

1. Beloved I AM (3x)
2. By God's violet ray (3x)

3. By God's love ray (3x)
4. It's done today, it's done to stay,
   it's done God's way (3x)

Interspersing songs with your decrees is a great way to feel the love and joy of the heavenly hosts. "Love to the Elementals" is a simple song that children like to sing to send their love and gratitude to the elementals. The words are sung to the tune of "My Bonnie Lies over the Ocean."

Love to the Elementals

We love you, we love you, we love you
Our dear elementals, we do
All beings of air, fire and water
And beings of earth, we love you.
I AM Presence, free all elementals
The great, the small
I AM Presence, through them
Give protection to all!

A Plea from the Elementals

*T*he nature spirits count on the children of God for the violet flame they need. The hierarchs governing these forces of nature have reiterated that the elementals are heavily bowed down with the burdens of mankind's karma and the pollution of the elements. Therefore, they've emphasized the importance of daily calling forth the violet flame for those in the nature kingdom who serve to sustain our environment.

> *Invoke the violet flame on behalf of the elementals who support the very foundation of your existence....*
>
> *The future can be bright if you... visualize and direct... your violet flame calls into the earth body on behalf of not only the gnomes but also the fiery salamanders, the sylphs of the air and the undines of the water.*
>
> — HIERARCHS OF THE EARTH ELEMENT

Without the sea and its many life-supporting functions…, earth could no longer be considered viable as an ecosystem or an evolutionary platform for its present lifewaves….

Let the sacred-fire action of the violet flame restore the natural flow of Spirit and Spirit's fire to provide the alchemy of transmutation within the seas, without which there can be no return to balance. And then let scientists, futurists, students and concerned citizens en masse rise up to defend the purity and power, the light and the jeweled crystal, the beauty and the bounty of our eternal sea.

— HIERARCHS OF THE WATER ELEMENT

We come to announce to you that elemental life must have a greater reinforcement of the violet flame. This you can do in fifteen to twenty minutes daily. And in that confined manifestation, you may see world transmutation and a new enlightenment for all people who have the desire to possess it.

— HIERARCHS OF THE EARTH ELEMENT

PART 8

True Stories of Encounters with Elementals

From Adults with Childlike Eyes

Elementals in the Flowers

Mark Prophet described how the elementals like to play among the flowers.

You can go into some of the sylvan glens in Ireland as well as in the United States, and you can see with spiritual vision some of these elementals.... They'll be down here with a nasturtium or a rose bush. You may see this elemental who may be no higher than two or three inches. He will dance and pirouette around.

Then he'll suddenly leap into the air like the ballerinas do, and he'll go up and cling to the very edge of a little branch right over a rose. And then he may fasten his legs on the branch, and he will hang down. In other words, he'll hang head down over a rose.

*And he'll reach down into it and he'll sniff
the essence of the rose, just like people will
smell a flower. Then the little elemental
will suddenly go around the other way, and
he'll leap gracefully.*

*The elementals do this to the tune of
music. They have their own musical instru-
ments, and they create many beautiful
melodies.*

A Friendly Tree Elemental

Of course elementals like to be in the trees, as
this traveler discovered when she was passing by.

*Sometimes I travel long distances alone in
my car when I'm on vacation. One time as
I was driving along, I was on a two-lane
highway that was not too busy. Ahead of me
was an old, rather barren-looking tree curving
over toward the shoulder, very close to the
road. I couldn't help but notice a tree elemental leaning out through the tree. He was smil-
ing broadly and waving emphatically at me as
I was approaching.*

*Making sure that there was no other car
very near me, I waved and smiled back until
I passed him. He seemed to be happy that
I acknowledged his presence. It felt very nice
to have such an enthusiastic, enjoyable experience with this friendly tree elemental.*

A Gnome Who Helped with the Dishes

This little gnome just wanted to work.

I used to have a little gnome help me wash
dishes and pots. Before he ever started, he
had spent a long time sitting on a small shelf
watching me. Upon noticing him, I asked
him what he was doing there and what his
name was.

He said, "My name is Ra Moose and I'm
tough as nails, and I am watching you do the
dishes."

I asked, "Why don't you come down and
help me?"

He said, "Because you haven't asked
me to!"

A Lesson in Kindness

A young elemental taught this assuming lady
a valuable lesson.

*I have always been able to see nature spirits,
and one day I saw one sitting next to me
while I was driving. I looked at the gnome
and instructed him to tell me his name in
fifteen minutes.*

*When I asked for the name, the being
told me "Precious." Associating that name
with the creature from the Tolkien trilogy
and assuming that this gnome was masculine,
I reacted rather rudely. In fact, I told the
gnome that name was really bad and he had
another fifteen minutes to "get it right."*

*The next time I asked, a tiny, nervous
voice squeaked out that she was a girl and she
just couldn't help that her name was Precious.
Her voice was so sad and hurt that I was immediately contrite and apologized profusely.*

*I learned from my interchange with
Precious that day (she is now my very best*

friend and helper) that we must be kind and gentle with all elemental life. "Rough and ready" was not the order of the day!

A Magnificent Mountain Being

Some of mankind's usually unseen helpers are large and towering beings.

Many years ago, my mother and I were driving from Kansas City to Colorado Springs. Western Kansas is pretty flat, you know, and I was so excited to see mountains in the far distance after so many miles of straight, flat driving. In my excitement, I started shouting greetings to the "gods of the mountains." I kept this up for miles, much to my mother's annoyance.

Finally, we got close enough to see Pike's Peak pretty clearly. Suddenly, I saw what looked like a huge being standing up over the peak! I thought I must be hallucinating. But just then, my mother calmly said, "Now you've done it. You've waked him up."

I felt a thrilling and enormous energy,
a definite vibration of welcome to it, so
I greeted the magnificent being graciously.

A Special Wind on a Still Day

It's in the invisible but distinct stirrings in nature that the elementals often make themselves known.

I *work as a recycling truck driver in Minneapolis. We all work as one-man teams. We have rhythm in everything we do and I think of my work as a cosmic rhythm.*

Sometimes cans that fall out of the recycling truck will roll under it. I used to crawl under the truck or pull it forward, then get down and pick up the can. Either way, this broke my rhythm.

The elementals realize that there is a rhythm to life and they keep me in that rhythm. I just have to call to them, "I need that can. Blow it back to me," and they do it.

Yesterday was a windless day. The air was quiet and still. A can fell under the truck

*where I couldn't reach it. Before I could even
ask, the can blew forcefully back to me.*

 # Hearts That Still Believe

Fairies and Fireflies

When she was a girl, this lady described, she
could see the elementals.

When I was young, my life was like a fairy
tale. I could see the fairies and other beings
of nature, and I thought everyone saw them.
I often visited my grandmother, who lived out
in the country where there are no streetlights.
At night I would watch the fairies flying with
the fireflies. I would sing to them. They love
singing!

Giggling in the Night

Late one night, this schoolgirl was awakened
by the sounds of some playful elementals.

While living in Canada, at the age of seven, one school night I went to bed and woke up later to the sound of giggling. I saw three elementals happily jumping around on my bed. At one point, it was as if one of them was peeking down at my face waving at me from a height of about four feet, as though he was looking over a box.

It was obvious that the elementals wanted to play with me. But I had school the next day and mentally told them that I had to go to sleep so I could get up in the morning.

With that, I threw the covers over my head and soon fell asleep, ignoring them. It was much easier in those days to fall asleep no matter what was going on, even giggling.

Elementals Can't Make Up for Carelessness

When she was a little girl, this woman learned an important lesson about the elementals.

I especially loved the trees as a child, and in spite of now living where there are few, I still love trees most of all plant life. The stories they tell are marvelous. They are real people to me, and as a child I loved being held in their arms.

One day I slipped and slid down the trunk of a very small tree. My tummy was scraped raw. I felt betrayed by my tree friend, whom I thought should have prevented me from falling and getting hurt, and I sobbed for hours.

When I finally told my mother why I was so upset, she explained that the tree was not at fault. That day, with her patient help, I learned that I had to take into account the properties of the physical world when I was climbing trees or wading in the creek.

My mother explained that if I was careless and slipped, the nature spirits could not keep me from falling. Even so, she said she always asked the angels and the nature beings to guard us as we played about the farm.

A Little Boy Learns to Call the Wind

Sometimes people learn about the elementals in their own special way.

I remember the time my mother taught me how to summon the wind.

We were at the ancestral home during summer break. As a young boy of nine, I enjoyed coming to the province where my mother grew up. The local household helpers loved to entertain me with stories of nature spirits, both malevolent and benign, and folklore tales handed down from the mountain dwellers.

This particular summer was terribly hot. Not even the cooler waters of the South China Sea could bring relief.

"It's so hot . . . It's too hot to go to the beach," I lamented.

My mother readily responded: "So, let's just call the wind." She drew herself up, paused, puckered her lips and whistled.

It was a simple whistle. It started with a mid-range note and ended with a trailing higher note. It was airy and light. I imagined myself being carried away on that fading tone. She whistled a couple of times, not hurriedly, but steadily. It was a calming sound.

Soon the outdoors started to stir. The leaves rustled gently and the wide-open windows of the sala (living room) let in a gentle breeze. She called the wind a few more times just for fun.

I learned to whistle that summer. And I've used that technique to call the wind ever since.

Fairies in the Violets and Bouncing Bettys

Another little girl discovered that someone very close to her knew the fairies, just like she did.

When I was a little girl, I lived on a farm with no TV and hardly any radio. I spent many hours playing in the garden of earth. My favorite place was behind the barn by the spring, where many purple and white violets grew. There were also lovely amethyst-colored flowers, known as Bouncing Bettys,

because they bounced in the breezes,
I thought. I talked to the fairies I saw there
and, indeed, I talked to everything that
lived—especially trees but also the pigs,
cows, horses and chickens.

One afternoon when I came in from
playing, my mother asked me where I had
been. When I told her, "By the spring, in the
violets," she exclaimed, "I love that spot!
Have you been talking to the fairies?"

I said yes, and she told me, "I always
loved to play in the violets best of all. I've
noticed that there are always many more
fairies where the violets grow than anywhere
else. When I was little," she continued, "I had
a special place where there was a big rock
shaped like a chair, up on the hill above the
railroad station. It was in a huge field of
violets and Bouncing Bettys. I always saw
more fairies there than anywhere else."

I was so pleased that my mother saw the
fairies too! I was never told that fairies did
not exist, and so I have seen them and talked
to them all my life.

PART 9

More Calls for Divine Intervention

Decrees to Archangel Michael

Whenever you need protection—every day as you go about your life or in times of climatic and earth changes—you can call on Archangel Michael. This mighty archangel is the Captain of the Lord's Hosts and he has unlimited legions of angels in his command. When we call for his protection, he is at our side.

In prayer sessions to the violet flame, decrees to Archangel Michael are usually given first. After giving the tube of light decree, you can invoke the protection of Archangel Michael with the following decree. As you give it, see Archangel Michael in your mind's eye standing before you arrayed in armour of light. See him guarding you, your loved ones and all elemental life from all negative conditions and harm.

Archangel Michael's Blue-Flame Armour

In the name of the beloved Presence of God, I AM in me, beloved Archangel Michael and your legions of blue-flame angels, I call for the protection of myself, my loved ones, my nation, the earth and all elemental life. And I accept it done according to the will of God.

1. Lord Michael, Lord Michael,
   I call unto thee—
   Wield thy sword of blue flame
   And now cut me free!

Refrain:* Blaze God-power, protection
   Now into my world,
   Thy banner of faith
   Above me unfurl!
   Transcendent blue lightning
   Now flash through my soul,
   I AM by God's mercy
   Made radiant and whole!

2. Lord Michael, Lord Michael,
   I love thee, I do—
   With all thy great faith
   My being imbue!

*Give the refrain once after each verse.

3. Lord Michael, Lord Michael
   And legions of blue—
   Come seal me, now keep me
   Faithful and true!

Coda:　　I AM with thy blue flame
　　　　　Now full-charged and blest,
　　　　　I AM now in Michael's
　　　　　Blue-flame armour dressed! (3x)

Fortify yourself, your loved ones and the elementals with calls to Archangel Michael by giving the following "Traveling Protection" decree three times or as many times as you want. If you don't have time to say this decree in the morning (either at your altar or while you're getting ready for the day), you can recite it aloud as you drive to work, give it quietly as you walk to your destination, or say it silently as you ride the bus or subway.

Visualize Archangel Michael and his legions as majestic angels arrayed in shining armour and wearing capes of brilliant sapphire blue, the color that carries the vibration and energy of protection. See them placing their magnificent presence around you, your family, your friends, the elementals and all those for whom you are praying.

Traveling Protection

Lord* Michael before,
Lord Michael behind,
Lord Michael to the right,
Lord Michael to the left,
Lord Michael above,
Lord Michael below,
Lord Michael, Lord Michael wherever I go!

I AM his love protecting here!
I AM his love protecting here!
I AM his love protecting here!

Reversing Negative Conditions

The powerful decree "Reverse the Tide" can be used in many types of natural disasters and other situations. After giving the preamble, use one of the previously suggested prayers for the elementals or compose your own prayer for the specific situation you are dealing with.

Lord is used in this prayer as a term of honor, denoting that Archangel Michael carries the power and presence of God.

Give the body of the decree, preferably while standing, with your hands raised and your palms facing out. Visualize the legions of light reversing the tide of any negative energies that may be working through the situation.

Reverse the Tide

In the name of the beloved mighty victorious Presence of God, I AM in me, my Higher Self, beloved Elohim, Archangel Michael and all elemental life—fire, air, water, and earth! I decree:

> Reverse the tide! (3x)
> Roll them back! (3x)
> Reverse the tide! (3x)
>   Take thy command!
> Roll them back! (3x)
> Set all free! (3x)
> Reverse the tide! (3x)*
>
> Unite the people in liberty! (3x)
> By God's own love now set them free! (3x)
> Unite the earth and keep it free (3x)
> By each one's I AM victory! (3x)

---

*Repeat this stanza 3, 12 or 36 times.

Expanding the Light of the Sun

Helios and Vesta

To the Beings Who Ensoul the Sun

Helios and Vesta!
Helios and Vesta!
Helios and Vesta!
Let the light flow into my being!
Let the light expand in the center
   of my heart!
Let the light expand in the center
   of the earth
And let the earth be transformed
   into the New Day!

Invincible Protection of the Light I AM!

Invincible protection of the light I AM!
Invincible protection of the light I command!
Invincible protection of the light is mine each day!
Invincible protection of the light
   through me forever hold sway!

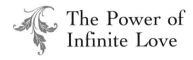

The Power of Infinite Love

I AM the Light of the Heart

I AM the light of the heart
Shining in the darkness of being
And changing all into
The golden treasury
Of the mind of Christ.

I AM projecting my love
Out into the world
To erase all errors
And to break down all barriers.

I AM the power of infinite love,
Amplifying itself
Until it is victorious,
World without end!

An Opportunity to Help Elemental Life

Each and every one of us has potentially millions of elementals who depend on us. They depend on us to pray for them, to offer violet flame for them. Considering the cataclysmic events that have already occurred in recent years, surely it is in our best interest to remember the elementals, to walk and talk with them, to pray to their hierarchs and to encourage them, to give them hope and stand by them.

The elementals have helped us for so long. Now we have an opportunity to help them—and we have the spiritual tools to do it. Through the divine spark within our heart, we can call forth divine assistance for lifting the burdens of Mother Nature and bringing renewal to all elemental life on planet Earth.

Will you do it? Will you commit to helping the nature spirits? What will you do to heal and renew our planet and elemental life?

*W*e would love to hear about
your efforts and victories on behalf of
elemental life and planet Earth.

You can write us at
info@SummitUniversityPress.com.

ADDITIONAL RESOURCES

CDS AND IMAGES

**Devotions, Decrees and Spirited Songs
to Archangel Michael**
by Elizabeth Clare Prophet
1 CD with booklet introductory pace #D93090

Save the World with Violet Flame #1
by Saint Germain
2 CDs with booklet introductory pace #D88019

Archangel Michael (stained-glass portrait)
Wallet card full color #3581

Violet Flame
Wallet card full color #2944

Chart of Your Divine Self
2⅛" x 3⅝" full color #1060

BOOKS AND BOOKLETS

I Am Your Guard:
How Archangel Michael Can Protect You
by Elizabeth Clare Prophet
Pocket guide 144 pages #7268

How to Work with Angels
by Elizabeth Clare Prophet
Pocket guide 118 pages #4445

Violet Flame to Heal Body, Mind and Soul
by Elizabeth Clare Prophet
Pocket guide 100 pages #4424

The Creative Power of Sound:
Affirmations to Create, Heal and Transform
by Elizabeth Clare Prophet
Pocket guide 107 pages #4447

The Story of Your Soul
by Elizabeth Clare Prophet
Pocket guide 136 pages #7276

Lost Teachings on Finding God Within
The Lost Teachings of Jesus series
by Mark L. Prophet and Elizabeth Clare Prophet
Pocketbook 352 pages #6365

Heart, Head and Hand Decrees
Booklet 48 pages #4444

Angels
Booklet of prayers, decrees and mantras
18 pages #3600

To place an order or request a free catalog, please contact:
Summit University Press, 63 Summit Way,
Gardiner, MT 59030-9314 USA
1-800-245-5445 or 406-848-9500
www.SummitUniversityPress.com
www.PocketGuidesToPracticalSpirituality.com

SUMMIT UNIVERSITY 🜨 PRESS®

POCKET GUIDES TO
PRACTICAL SPIRITUALITY SERIES

I Am Your Guard:
How Archangel Michael Can Protect You

The Story of Your Soul:
Recovering the Pearl of Your True Identity

Karma and Reincarnation

Alchemy of the Heart:
How to Give and Receive More Love

Your Seven Energy Centers:
A Holistic Approach to Physical,
Emotional and Spiritual Vitality

The Art of Practical Spirituality:
How to Bring More Passion, Creativity
and Balance into Everyday Life

Soul Mates and Twin Flames

How to Work with Angels

Access the Power of Your Higher Self

The Creative Power of Sound:
Affirmations to Create, Heal and Transform

Creative Abundance:
Keys to Spiritual and Material Prosperity

Violet Flame to Heal Body, Mind and Soul

POCKET GUIDES TO PRACTICAL SPIRITUALITY

SUMMIT UNIVERSITY 🔥 PRESS®

I Am Your Guard
How Archangel Michael Can Protect You
by Elizabeth Clare Prophet

Terrorism. War. Earth changes. Violent crime. The threats to our families, nations and environment are enormous. Now more than ever, we need Archangel Michael. This breakthrough book will introduce you to Archangel Michael and how you can call for his protection.

ISBN: 978-1-932890-12-9
112 pages $8.95

Revered in Jewish, Christian and Islamic traditions, Archangel Michael can protect you and your loved ones in times of trouble. Includes true-life stories of Archangel Michael's intercession.

How to Work with Angels
by Elizabeth Clare Prophet

Learn ten steps to make angels a part of your life.

"Whether for love, healing, protection, guidance or illumination, angels stand ready to help you in many practical and personal ways. And as Elizabeth Clare Prophet says, working with angels also puts us in touch with our higher self."

—BODHI TREE BOOK REVIEW

ISBN: 978-0-922729-41-8
118 pages $6.95

ISBN: 978-1-932890-11-2
136 pages $8.95

The Story of Your Soul
Recovering the Pearl of Your True Identity
by Elizabeth Clare Prophet

Who am I? Why am I here? Where am I going?… Some have likened the soul to a pearl cast into the sea of the material universe. The goal of our life is to go after that pearl and recover our true identity. *The Story of Your Soul* champions the profound worth and nobility of the individual. It is a story of awakening and overcoming. Includes: Seven keys for your soul's journey, personal stories, affirmations, meditations, visualizations, and reflective discussion questions.

Soul Mates and Twin Flames
The Spiritual Dimension of Love and Relationships
by Elizabeth Clare Prophet

"After thirty-five years as a relationship counselor, I find *Soul Mates and Twin Flames* to be extremely powerful in revealing the inner mysteries of the soul and the true essence of love through its insightful analysis of real-life experiences and classical love stories."

—MARILYN C. BARRICK, Ph.D.,
author of *Sacred Psychology of Love*

ISBN: 978-0-922729-48-7
164 pages $6.95

Violet Flame to Heal Body, Mind and Soul

by Elizabeth Clare Prophet

This pocket guide describes how to use a high-frequency, spiritual energy to increase vitality, overcome blocks to healing, dissolve records of trauma and create positive change in our personal lives and for the planet. Learn how the violet flame can be used to increase vitality and to assist any healing process of the body, mind, emotions or spirit.

ISBN: 978-0-922729-37-1
108 pages $8.95

Includes: Inspiring true stories, nine easy steps to begin using the violet flame with affirmations, mantras, and visualizations.

The Creative Power of Sound

Affirmations to Create, Heal and Transform
by Elizabeth Clare Prophet

Learn how to change our physical, mental, emotional and spiritual worlds with the power of sound. Seven fundamental principles for using affirmations, decrees, prayers and more. For centuries mystics of the East and West have believed that sound creates matter. This book shows that sound is the energy of creation and explains how to experiment with sound patterns in our lives.

ISBN: 978-0-922729-42-5
108 pages $8.95

Creative Abundance
Keys to Spiritual and Material Prosperity
by Elizabeth Clare Prophet and Mark L. Prophet

ISBN: 978-0-922729-38-8
174 pages $8.95

"*Creative Abundance* contains keys for magnetizing the spiritual and material abundance we all need. Its sensible step-by-step techniques—including treasure mapping, principles of feng shui, meditations, visualizations and affirmations—show how to live a full and prosperous life."

—BODHI TREE BOOK REVIEW

Karma and Reincarnation
Transcending Your Past, Transforming Your Future
by Elizabeth Clare Prophet with Patricia R. Spadaro

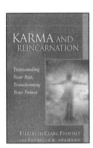

ISBN: 978-0-922729-61-6
224 pages $6.95

The word *karma* has made it into the mainstream. But not everyone understands what it really means or how to deal with it. This insightful book will help you come to grips with karmic connections from past lives that have helped create the circumstances of your life today. You'll discover how your actions in past lives—good and bad—affect which family you're born into, who you're attracted to, and why some people put you on edge. You'll learn about group karma, what we do between lives, and how to turn your karmic encounters into grand opportunities to shape the future you want.

To order call 1-800-245-5445.

Elizabeth Clare Prophet is a world-renowned author. Among her bestselling titles are *Fallen Angels and the Origins of Evil, The Lost Years of Jesus,* The Lost Teachings of Jesus series, *Kabbalah: Key to Your Inner Power, Reincarnation: The*

Missing Link in Christianity, and her Pocket Guides to Practical Spirituality series, which includes *Your Seven Energy Centers, Karma and Reincarnation, The Story of Your Soul,* and *Violet Flame to Heal Body, Mind and Soul.*

She has pioneered techniques in practical spirituality, including the creative power of sound for personal growth and world transformation.

A wide selection of her books is available worldwide in approximately 30 languages. Mrs. Prophet retired in 1999 and is now living in Montana's Rocky Mountains. The unpublished works of Mark L. Prophet and Elizabeth Clare Prophet continue to be published by Summit University Press.